THE ROYAL HORTICULTURAL SOCIETY

NIGEL COLBORN

WISLEY

inspiration for all seasons

PHOTOGRAPHED BY
CLAY PERRY

First published in 2006 by
The Royal Horticultural Society
80 Vincent Square
London SW1P 2PE

Registered Charity number 222879

www.rhs.org.uk

A CIP catalogue record for this book is available
from the British Library.

ISBN 1-902896-67-X

Edited by Simon Maughan
Designed by Paul Welti
Colour reproduction by Phoenix Colour, Leicester
Printed and bound in the UK by Cambridge
Printing, Cambridge

With thanks to all the staff at Wisley

contents

introduction

Nothing can prevent a great garden from working its magic. Inspiration calls from every corner and even the most knowledgeable gardeners are likely to see plants they have never come across before. Non-gardeners, too, can expect to be wooed, not only by verdant landscapes and pleasing colours but also by the sense of peace and tranquillity. There are bewitching fragrances to savour, from lilies or old roses in high summer, to winter daphnes or spring jonquils. Natural sounds enhance the experience, too, be they birdsong, bees working in the blossoms, wind sighing in the pines or even the hiss and rustle of dry grasses moving in midwinter wind.

(PRECEDING PAGE) Spring bedding, with tulips and wall-flowers, looking towards the main entrance. Hornbeam is the favoured hedging material in this part of the garden.

(RIGHT) In the foreground, *Iris sibirica* 'Caesar's Brother' – a garden variety of the eastern European species – decorates the margin of the Rock Garden stream with *Iris pseudacorus*, our native yellow flag, behind.

(OPPOSITE) Early growth in the pebbly Grass Border with the golden variegated blades of *Hakonechloa macra* 'Aureola' making a bright contrast with the darker green, emerging leaves of the hybrid *Agapanthus* 'Blue Bird'. In the background, the fleshy, blue-green foliage of *Sedum spectabile* 'Brilliant' makes neat, almost spherical shapes.

In such a large acreage – Wisley's runs to 24 hectares (60 acres) – and with so much going on, the most frequent mistake is to underestimate the time needed to get the best out of your visit. This is truly a garden for everyone, with bedding displays, traditional borders, revolutionary planting schemes, model gardens, grass borders, water features, plant trials, immaculate lawns, flowery meadows, rock gardens, Mediterranean gardens, rose gardens, herb gardens and so much more. A stroll along the banks of the River Wey, for example, could enable wildlife enthusiasts to spot a kingfisher; soft fruit growers can marvel at the cordon gooseberries; whereas those who regret the passing of historic techniques can admire the carpet bedding, newly styled every spring.

(LEFT) Echinaceas, perovskias and phlomis dominate the colour range in the Glasshouse Borders in August.

(RIGHT) Foxtail lily, *Eremurus* 'Joanna', by the Walled Gardens, bordering the main path that leads to the Bicentenary Glasshouse.

You will find innovation here, side by side with time-honoured practices and traditional styles. The current craze for growing tropical plants outdoors, for example, is carried out *par excellence* in several parts of the garden, and when you stand atop the Fruit Mount, to look down towards the vast Bicentenary Glasshouse, opening in 2007, you will be able to enjoy the soft planting and gentle colours of the Glasshouse Borders, stretching away in the middle distance. These represent an entirely novel approach to naturalistic planting with herbaceous grassland species.

A great deal more is going on, in this great garden, than meets the eye of a casual visitor. In the Laboratory Building, RHS scientists and gardening experts deal with over 65,000 enquiries every year and are frequently the first to discover pests and diseases new to British plants.

Students work and study here and the two libraries are in constant use. The Herbarium holds thousands of dried plant specimens and Wisley's repository of literature on horticultural taxonomy is the world's most comprehensive. The latest techniques are deployed here, too, and current gardening trends and fashions are also put to the test. New approaches, however, are always made to go hand in hand with sustainable gardening practice, and with care for the environment.

Changing times, during its hundred-year history, brought major challenges to Wisley. Two World Wars forced change and the 1987 and 1990 storms created new planting opportunities. Future issues on climate change, energy use and increasing shortage of water will also need to be addressed, but whatever the future holds, this enchanting garden is here in the now, to visit, to treasure, and to enjoy throughout the seasons.

(ABOVE) The red clay tile roof and Elizabethan style belies the true age of the Laboratory Building, which is just under a century. Construction work began in 1914 and was completed in 1916. The design was deliberately chosen to appear as if the garden had been developed around the Laboratory, rather than preceding it. The Canal in the foreground leads from the Loggia.

(OPPOSITE) A sweet gum, *Liquidambar styraciflua*, in late autumn.

spring

spring bulbs

What could be more uplifting, on a balmy spring day, than hearing a cuckoo calling above a fragrant drift of bluebells? Flowering bulbs make a colourful and often fragrant contribution to any spring garden, whether formally bedded or allowed to naturalise. Their flowering period may be brief but their colours are usually bright and cheerful, and the value to early bees is substantial. Furthermore, most species have the grace to die away discreetly, after their season, making way for summer plants.

Bluebells in the wild are under threat, not only from habitat loss and damage by feral deer, but also because of the introduced Spanish relative *Hyancinthoides hispanica* with which they are prone to hybridise.

Bluebells (*Hyacinthoides non-scripta*) naturalised under silver birches in the Wild Garden. This species is a key constituent of the ancient woodland flora, thriving in dappled shade and deep soils, rich in leaf-mould.

(TOP) In March or April, broad drifts of daffodils and narcissi, plus a rich miscellany of other spring bulbs, will make your garden walk a truly memorable experience.

(ABOVE) A close relative of the anemone, *Hepatica nobilis* has three-lobed leaves and gem-like flowers in sky blue, pink or purplish shades. Both scientific and colloquial name, liverwort, refers to the roots, which resemble a mammalian liver.

(LEFT) In favourable conditions, bluebells will naturalise freely among introduced plants, provided the balance of soil-borne micro-organisms is undamaged, by fertilisers, for example. Here, the variegated foliage of *Hosta fortunei* var. *albo-picta* makes a cheerful contrast with the fragrant flowers.

Glorious tulips in rude health! More than 60 varieties grow here, from mid-season Darwin hybrids to late Parrot types, with their feathered petals. After flowering, the bed is cleared to make way for the sub-tropical planting, illustrated on pages 94–95.

spring blossom

Apple blossom is pretty enough to feature
in the most ornamental of gardens, its trusses
of coral buds opening to pale pink or white
flowers with lemon stamens. But when the
trees have been professionally pruned and
trained, that beauty is further enhanced by
promise of a bountiful harvest. Along the
entrance to the Fruit Field, trees are pruned in
a variety of ways, showing cordon techniques,
for example, and fan training. The skill, to
retain the desired shape and productivity of
such trees, is not difficult to acquire but calls
for considerable time and patience.

(BELOW) Mid-season
dessert apple 'Sunset'
and late dessert apple
'Ashmead's Kernel' fan-
trained on horizontal wires.

(RIGHT) The five-petalled
flowers of apple 'Sunset'.

water's edge

Damp soils take longer to warm up in spring than do sunny banks or sheltered woodland, so waterside flowers tend not to appear until well into the season. What they lack in timeliness, however, is more than made up for by their spectacular qualities. Some species produce their flowers first, to be followed later by huge, lush leaves that dominate the wetland vegetation. The lysichitons are typical of such plants, producing low-growing spathes in spring, followed by vast, oar-shaped leaves. Siberian irises grow more modestly and are suitable to grace a border as well as a natural bog. They bring cheerful colour in late spring or early summer, but they keep their narrow, sword-like foliage fresh throughout the growing season.

(OPPOSITE) Where the Alpine Meadow runs down to the Wild Garden near the Long Ponds, a drift of *Iris sibirica* 'Heavenly Blue' brightens the foreground with South American bamboo *Chusquea culeou* behind and low-growing Japanese maples in fresh new foliage.

The flowers of saxifrage relative *Darmera peltata*, emerging among wood anemone foliage. Huge leaves will follow on 2-metre stems.

The flowers of *Lysichiton camtschatcensis*, a northeastern Asian species, precedes its large leaves.

Silver edges on the falls (lower petals) of *Iris sibirica* 'Heavenly Blue' help to accent the intense flower colour.

By mid-spring, growth towards the midsummer climax is reaching maximum speed. Within a few warm days the ferns at the entrance to the Rock Garden's grotto – as yet tightly furled in fiddlehead shapes – begin to expand and develop graceful fronds of fresh, pale green. Native to Britain, ostrich feather ferns, *Matteuccia struthiopteris* (bottom left of main picture), assume the shapes of big green shuttlecocks; behind them, the American cinnamon fern, *Osmunda cinnamomea*, carries its leaves on longer stalks and has separate, spore-bearing stems. The bold foliage of *Rodgersia podophylla* forms a mantle over the grotto.

(BELOW) The grotto in mid-spring, when the flowers of *Darmera peltata* develop ahead of the foliage.

(RIGHT) A few weeks later the ferns are now well developed, and the rodgersia is coming into bloom.

A rustic bridge crosses the Long Ponds, connecting the
Alpine Meadow and Rock Garden with the Wild Garden.
A pause midstream, here, will enable you to gaze at flowers
and foliage reflected in the water. Assorted rhododendrons
provide splashes of colour, and on the bridge itself the long
racemes of *Wisteria floribunda* 'Multijuga' hang down to the
surface of the water. The flowers of the lysichiton are over by
now, but their huge leaves make an architectural statement
along the edge.

(LEFT) The fresh, brightly coloured flowers and luxuriant vegetation that borders the stream makes a startling contrast with last year's dead stems of common reed, *Phragmites communis*, in the left-hand background.

(RIGHT) Wisley's Alpine Meadow is at its loveliest in April, when the turf is full of hoop petticoat daffodils, *Narcissus bulbocodium*. Snakeshead fritillaries, dog's tooth violets and several crocus species also grow in the meadow grass.

floral jewel case

The Alpine Display House is at its best in early spring when so many small plants pack such a large punch of colour and character. Alpine pots or pans, containing specimen plants, are plunged into a grit substrate to create a natural-looking display, despite their diverse origins. Orchid species of *Pleione*, from South East Asia, rub shoulders with cyclamen from the southern Mediterranean and trilliums from North America.

(ABOVE) A pan of hybrid *Pleione* Tongariro gx. Pleiones are mountain plants occurring wild from Nepal to China. Most of the hybrids have been developed from the hardiest species, *Pleione formosana*, a native of Taiwan.

(ABOVE) *Oxalis enneaphylla* 'Ruth Tweedie', a selected form of a Patagonian species so named because the blue-green leaves are deeply divided, supposedly, into eleven parts. It is hardy in Britain, but will benefit from good drainage.

(OPPOSITE) The distinctive crimson-edged buds of *Oxalis versicolor*, which open to white flowers. The protection of an Alpine house is essential for this South African sorrel whose leaves are divided into three leaflets.

(ABOVE) A *Lewisia cotyledon* hybrid. These short-lived perennials have been crossed to produce hybrids with flowers in colours ranging from yellow and orange, through peachy and salmon tones to rich pink.

SPRING PRIMULAS

In the eighteenth century, breeding fancy flowers was a passion shared by several artisan communities. Some of their most exquisitely bred specimens have survived to the present day, or have given rise to progeny that has similar qualities. The European primula, particularly *Primula auricula*, was especially prized and continues to be a popular exhibition plant.

Florists, as the artisans came to be known, strove to develop particular characteristics in auriculas. Green in the

petals, seen in 'Moselle' (above), was much sought-after, as was the pleasing, disc-shaped flowers and subtle colours of the light-centred alpines (above left). 'Harry Hotspur' (right) has a large, white centre, with fine colour grading on the outer petals.

Oxlips *Primula elatior*, cowslips *P. veris*, and primroses *P. vulgaris* were also hybridised to develop distinctive strains. Gold laced polyanthus (bottom left) were much loved by the Victorians and are still deservedly popular.

cacti

True cacti, all from the New World, are adapted for coping with extreme conditions. Their fleshy stems store water, for use during prolonged drought, and the almost complete absence of leaves enables them to function with significantly less moisture than required by most green plants. Spines and prickles help to protect them from predation by herbivores and many are clothed with fine, silky hairs or down, which helps to protect them from extremes of heat. A strikingly similar adaptation has occurred independently in Old World plants, such as aloes and many euphorbias, which also grow in arid conditions.

(LEFT) Many cactus species, such the old lady cactus (*Mammilaria hahniana*) flower during spring, often with startlingly bright colours.

(RIGHT) The Mexican *Mammilaria haagiana* produces clusters of sausage-shaped stems and also has shocking pink flowers in spring.

battleston hill

The garden's highest point, Battleston Hill, is, not unnaturally, one of its windiest sites. It was here in October 1987 that an exceptionally strong gale laid waste most of the mature woodland. But what seemed disastrous, at first, proved a blessing – albeit very well disguised at the time. Aged or weakened trees were gone and many shrubs were ruined, but in their place lay a new opportunity. Earlier mistakes had been absolved overnight and once the debris had been cleared, a blank canvas was ready for new, creative planting.

Spring brings the brightest colours to this stretch of open woodland with magnolias, rhododendrons and camellias in the rose red, pink, and white range, all harmonising with the taller conifers and young broadleaf trees.

(LEFT) *Magnolia* x *soulangeana* 'Rustica Rubra', one of many excellent and moderately lime-tolerant cultivars resulting from the cross between *M. denudata* and *M. liliiflora*.

(RIGHT) An open, airy view of the gale-cleared Battleston Hill, with yellow-flowered *Magnolia* 'Elizabeth' (left) above Loderi rhododendrons, Scots pine in the background and, to the right, *Rhododendron* 'Bassett Beauty'.

(ABOVE) The evergreen azalea *Rhododendron* 'Beattie' growing in the Queen Mother's Walk, with *R.* 'Silver Sixpence', white, behind. The sculpture at the top of the walk, *Naissance* by Donald Foxley, was replaced in November 2005 with a Henry Moore.

(ABOVE) Looking towards the Model Gardens from Battleston Hill.

(LEFT) One of the many grassy paths leading from Battleston Hill to the Queen Mother's Walk, with *Betula utilis* var. *jacquemontii* in the foreground.

Azaleas and rhododendrons, looking down from the Queen Mother's Walk (above), include the light pink 'Patricia's Day' and, in the middle distance, the rosy purple Kurume azalea 'Hatsugiri'. English oaks, *Quercus robur*, preside over the shrubs, which are interplanted with herbaceous species for later interest. The winding turf pathway makes an attractive, informal setting, bordered by cooler, restful greens when the spring blossoms have fallen.

(LEFT) A mulched pathway winds its way around the woodland of Battleston Hill.

(BELOW) A mature specimen of the hybrid *Rhododendron* 'Bow Bells', whose handsome dome shape and compact size make it ideal as a 'structure shrub' in a mixed border.

The main attraction of Battleston Hill in spring is the collection of slow-growing hybrid rhododendrons. In the foreground of the main picture, for example, the red-flowered 'Hinode-no-taka' contrasts with creamy 'Carita Inchmery', and in the background (right) is a white form of the Himalayan species *R. campanulatum*. The central tree, *Ostrya japonica*, is a member of the birch family, related to the more widely known hop hornbeam, *O. carpinifolia*.

The rhododendron has played a key role in British gardens for more than 200 years. In the wild, there are more than 800 species, two-thirds of which have been grown, at some time or other, in the British Isles. These pure species have given rise, of course, to an even greater number of garden varieties. Though they occur in almost every continent, the great majority originate from Asia, in particular the Himalayas. Their culture goes back many centuries in the gardens of China and Japan, and in modern times *Rhododendron* is still one of the most planted genera worldwide.

(ABOVE LEFT) Detail of the award-winning hybrid *Rhododendron* 'Bow Bells', also illustrated on the previous page. The nodding, bell-shaped flowers, which hang in loose trusses, and spoon-shaped leaves are a feature of this variety.

(ABOVE) This close-up shows the typical features of a rhododendron flower. Many varieties have speckled pollen guides on their upper petals in contrasting colours.

There are tropical species to be found too, in the higher rain forests of South East Asia, but the majority prefer cool, moist conditions with high rainfall and a discrete, dormant winter period. This has made them popular in British gardens, particularly along our western side, where the climate is cooler and damper than in the east.

Rhododendrons at Wisley might not match up to those of the great Scottish or Cornish gardens, but the acid, sandy soil of Battleston Hill seems to suit a wide number of species, particularly the smaller, more resilient azaleas, such as the Kurume hybrids and deciduous kinds. These thrive, despite Surrey's relatively low rainfall.

Wallflowers *Erysimum cheiri* 'Blood Red' forms the bulk of this spring display, with the old variety 'Fire King' in the urns, along with *Euphorbia* x *martini*, blue-flowered anemones and primroses.

classic wisley

Summer bedding is already in flower at planting time, in May, but spring displays of wallflowers, forget-me-nots or bulbs must be planted half a year in advance.

The urns, on the path between the Canal and Seven Acres, bring form and structure to this spring bedding and provide an opportunity for extra plants. Strong colours are toned down by silver foliage and, in April sunshine, heat from the paving will bring out the wallflowers' sweet fragrance.

This unusual, double-flowered form of the familiar and much-loved climber, *Wisteria* x *formosa* 'Yae-kokuryu' is often labelled, incorrectly, as 'Black Dragon'. Despite its relative scarcity, culture is no more difficult that other wisterias.

Wisley is blessed with plenty of wall space, so it is not surprising that the collection of climbers and wall plants provides inspiration to gardeners. Among wisterias, for example, notable specimens include the large, white-flowered *W. brachybotrys*, which adorns the Loggia, by the Canal. Pruning, in both August and January, ensures optimum flowering, but even in mid-winter, the gnarled, twisting trunks provide character and interest to the garden's structure.

summer

the wild garden

In the Wild Garden, waterside shrubs and trees make cool shade and form a luxuriant background for bright summer perennials. Moisture-loving astilbes (bottom right) merge, here, with the startling magenta-flowered *Geranium psilostemon* (bottom left), which takes over from the gentler late spring hues of candelabra primulas. Closer to the stream, white arums and big, bold shocks of Bowles' golden sedge (*Carex elata* 'Aurea', centre), whose yellow foliage loses its intensity in summer, tumble towards the slow-moving water. This most naturalistic part of the garden is also its most historic for it was here, at the end of the nineteenth century, that George Fergusson Wilson began his Oakwood Experimental Garden.

Since its introduction to Britain, in 1731, the white arum lily, *Zantedeschia aethiopica*, has become so universally grown that its wild South African origins are almost forgotten. As a cut flower, this species is almost indispensable and it is increasingly popular as a container subject. Given the space, however, white arums are never more beautiful than when allowed to grow naturally, as they do in the Cape. Here in the Wisley wild garden, drifts of this large, handsome perennial have been allowed to develop along the waterside, enabling the flowers to be enjoyed in profusion among the bold foliage.

In colder regions, white arums need full protection from penetrating frost, but elsewhere, a thick, bulky mulch will usually suffice to bring the roots safely through an average winter.

midsummer rose gardens

Choicest midsummer jewel, in Wisley's crown, is the Golden Jubilee Rose Garden. Traditional beds, set in turf, are planted with a rich miscellany of hybrid roses in all shapes, sizes, colours and fragrances. Specimens here include the standard 'White Diamond' flowering above the curiously hued 'Rhapsody in Blue' with peachy salmon 'Razzle Dazzle' in the foreground.

In former times, rose gardens like this were widespread but fashions have changed and roses are usually grown in smaller numbers, by amateurs, often in association with other plants. The need for regular pruning and expert care makes them more demanding than most shrubs – hardly ideal for those whose busy lifestyle demands low-maintenance plants.

(ABOVE) The soft pinkish tones of *Rosa* 'Bantry Bay' in the foreground (left), with the standard-trained *R.* 'Bonica' at centre. The vigorous hybrid tea rose 'Pink Pearl' flowers below, along the front of the border.

The English Rose 'Brother Cadfael', bred by David Austin.

The rose theme continues across the path on Weather Hill, where the landscape is given over, not only to bedded shrub varieties but also to climbers and pillar roses. The soft pinkish tones provide seductive early summer colours and are especially beautiful when viewed in low light, either on an overcast day or during a long summer evening.

Managing roses *en masse*, like this, can be difficult. Most are susceptible to fungal diseases and to sap-sucking pests and it would be difficult to stage such an extensive display without professional management and rigorous attention to plant health. For amateur gardeners, pest and disease control has become far more difficult in recent years, following the withdrawal of so many efficacious fungicides and insecticides. Furthermore, many home owners prefer to garden without artificial chemicals these days. Such concerns, however, could never diminish the glory of Wisley's spectacular rose extravaganza.

The climber 'Arthur Bell'.

The old but dependable rambling variety 'Albertine'.

Another David Austin variety, 'Buttercup'.

WETLAND IRISES

The Japanese water iris, *Iris ensata*, is the most dramatic member of a diverse and colourful family. Wild forebears of *I. ensata* 'Barr Purple East' (opposite) grow in eastern Asia, but intensive breeding in Japan and elsewhere has resulted in garden varieties with colours that run from white, through deepening shades of blue or purple-red. Japanese water irises are happiest growing in or near water, or in deep, fertile, moisture-retentive soil. Flowering is spectacular but brief; the sword-like foliage persists all summer.

Less flamboyant than its Asian cousin, the wild yellow flag, *Iris pseudacorus* (below), is a familiar wetland plant of the British countryside. Garden selections include a variegated form, 'Variegata' and the primrose-yellow-flowered var. *bastardii*. The sturdy foliage and erect flower stems are important, at the water margin, for insects such as dragonfly nymphs, which climb out of the water to split their carapaces and emerge as adult dragonflies.

rock garden

For many visitors, the very heart of the
garden is right here. The great rock
bank, a convincing fragment
of mountain landscape,
takes bold, terraced
steps down to a
flower-strewn
Alpine meadow.

A near-perfect marriage exists, here, between the machinations of horticulture and natural beauty. The Rock Garden houses a manicured collection of dwarf shrubs and small trees, rock-loving perennials and tiny Alpine species, all arranged to create a naturalistic scene, despite the eclectic nature of the mix. In the meadow, exotic and native wildflowers are encouraged to self-seed, creating a rustic theme, which is echoed in the calm, slow-moving water of the Long Ponds that lie along the bottom of the valley. Here, native aquatic and marginal plants cohabit with exotic species and artificially bred cultivars.

(ABOVE) Even on a blowsy summer afternoon, rich planting on the Rock Garden gives a sense of lushness. Structure comes not only from the large rocks, but also from bold, evergreen conifers, with their distinctive upright or rounded shapes.

(OPPOSITE) The naturalistic Long Ponds where wild yellow water lily *Nuphar lutea*, bog bean *Menyanthes trifoliata* and yellow flag, *Iris pseudacorus*, make fitting companions to the moisture-loving Asian 'candelabra' primulas, seen in the foreground. Hot sunset colours, among wetland primulas, are derived from such species as *Primula bulleyana*, *P. chungensis* and the bright yellow *P. prolifera*. Pinks, crimsons and whites come from *P. japonica* and *P. pulverulenta*.

the container garden

One of Wisley's most useful Model Gardens is dedicated to growing plants exclusively in containers. With increasing pressure on space and shrinking garden sizes, many people have little choice, nowadays, but to do all their growing in pots, tubs or window boxes. This little garden, with its variety of containers, shows the diversity of plants that can adapt to pot culture.

POTS AND PLANTS

Using containers of different shapes, sizes and colours helps to sustain interest but also ensures that conditions are met for a wide range of plants. Tall pots, for example, are appreciated by antirrhinums, which like the long, cool root-run, as well as hostas, as they are more easily isolated from the attentions of slugs. Short containers may be interplanted with taller specimens so that a satisfying display can be achieved at both eye and ground level, and square containers give a different feel; their hard edges can be set against billowing or frothy flowers, ferny foliage or any other softly textured plant.

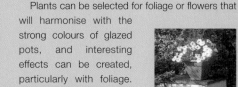

Plants can be selected for foliage or flowers that will harmonise with the strong colours of glazed pots, and interesting effects can be created, particularly with foliage. The deep purple, strap-like leaves of *Ophiopogon planiscapus* 'Nigrescens', for example, make a classic dark foil to almost any bright colour.

Petunia Surfinia Blue

Penstemon 'Burgundy'

Bidens ferulifolia

Argyranthemum
'Madeira São Martinho'

The Model Container Garden shows what can be done without a border, or even without natural soil in which to plant. Cheerful containerised summer displays like this are easy to achieve and here, colours and textures are sweetly composed for contrast and harmony. Most of the current colour comes from summer plants grown as annuals, but when their season is done, more permanent species, such as the potted blue fescue grass, *Festuca glauca*, and the dwarf New Zealand flax – just visible in the background – will continue to provide interest.

Current stars of the show, however, are the purple penstemon, blue petunia and pale double marguerite or argyranthemum, whose glaucous foliage makes a subtle colour contribution. These three, like the yellow-flowered, Mexican native *Bidens ferulifolia*, bloom constantly until mid-autumn. The penstemon is reasonably hardy and could over-winter safely, but few of the other plants would survive sustained frost.

glorious garlic In the Mixed Borders, *Allium christophii*, grown here with purple moor grass, *Molinia caerulea* subsp. *caerulea*, flowers in late spring with its globes of star-shaped, silvery mauve flowers, followed by long-lasting seed heads.

The pedicels (flower stalks) of *Allium schubertii* vary in length, giving the impression of an exploding star-burst firework, backed up here by the floriferous *Nepeta racemosa* 'Walker's Low'. There are roughly 700 other *Allium* species, many of which are highly decorative.

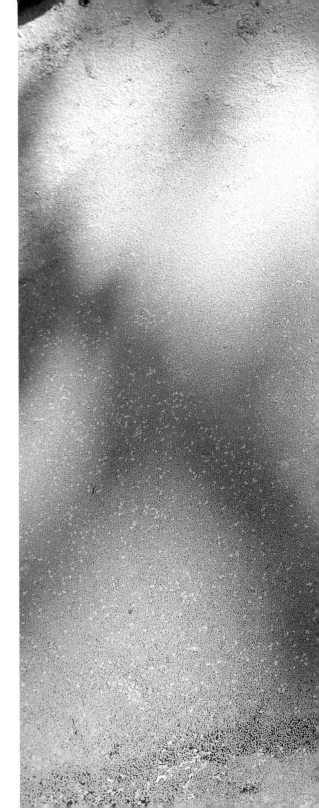

the canal

Formal water features bring a change of mood, contrasting with the floral abundance of the mixed borders and the exuberant vegetation of the wild garden. The rectangular Canal, above, runs from the Loggia to the mock Tudor Laboratory building seen in the background.

Running in line with the Canal, just behind the Walled Gardens, cascading water creates a pattern like a playing card 'spade' in the duckweed, *Lemna minor*, on the surface of a quiet pond. Some visitors throw coins into this feature, no doubt making a wish as they pass.

A calm, clear summer morning is perfect for viewing the formal water features. Foliage and flowers are at their freshest and the still waters reflect the outlines of the surrounding plants. The ruthless geometry of this design, with its straight sides, plumb corners and unforgiving lines is softened by the planting and brought to vibrant life by daring use of colour.

Abundant seats, here, enable one to rest awhile to enjoy the special ambience created by a large body of water. You might wish to spend time in a reflective mood while you relax in the morning sun but before long, you will want walk along the waterside and compare colours, flower size and growing habits of all the different water lilies that grow in the Canal. Expect no jumbled, Monet style of planting here! Instead, the water lilies are evenly spaced and labelled in large print, making it easy to note down varieties that impress, or that one might want to choose for a pond at home.

(LEFT) Still waters, where formal lines contrast with relaxed planting in the ponds at the 'Laboratory end' of the Canal. The Laboratory building is visible the background.

(ABOVE) Cannas, grown as aquatics, make bold reflections in the placid surface of ponds at one end of the Canal, which is bordered by a densely planted bank along its length.

In the borders that flank the water, the bright red *Penstemon* 'Andenken an Friedrich Hahn', formerly known at 'Garnet', and the vigorous and floriferous *Verbena* 'Homestead Purple' make a lively combination. Cannas, more frequently grown as border or container plants, show how happily they will thrive as aquatic plants. This tall yellow variety is Canna 'Ra'.

upholding a victorian tradition

In bygone years, almost every public park exhibited carpet bedding.
Now, few institutions can sustain such a labour-intensive practice,
but at Wisley the tradition continues. Designed and planted
annually, the current scheme is inspired by an historical, nine-
teenth-century illustration and realised by Wisley's Superintendent
of Glass, Nick Morgan.

The use of coloured plant material to create a living, growing tapestry calls for intricate skills, wise plant selection and almost eternal patience. In the past, garden apprentices were often detailed regularly to trim, sometimes with even with small scissors, the growing plants. Plank bridges must be suspended over the area, at planting time, to enable the artists to work.

a country garden

During the 1990s designer Penelope Hobhouse was commissioned to draw up plans for one of Wisley's larger enclosed areas where island beds were separated by turf. These were swept away to make room for the Country Garden where formal line and layout contrasts with relaxed underplanting. The area is intersected with broad, paved pathways along which wide arches give height and are furnished with Japanese wisteria. Formally pruned crab apples, *Malus* x *zumi* var. *calocarpa* 'Professor Sprenger' and M. *hupehensis*, are arranged evenly through the garden, and the modernistic water feature serves as a focal point.

Urban in its design, rather than rural, this is a garden whose strength lies in lush planting, which softens the hard landscaping. In early summer, blues and mauves predominate with spires of purple toad-flax, *Linaria purpurea*, in the foreground, delphiniums, and a few yellow mulleins. Rustic birch structures carry clematis while short-term plants such as *Smyrnium perfoliatum* are used to fill the spaces.

(LEFT) Green-flowered *Smyrnium perfoliatum* and conspicuous white umbels of *Cenolophium denudatum* paint a rural picture in the Country Garden. Both are members of the carrot family.

(ABOVE) Colours shift during
the year in the Country Garden,
but the purples and mauves, in
the foreground spires of *Linaria
purpurea* are the hues of high
summer.

One of the most dramatic
grasses in the Country Garden,
particularly in early summer, is
the golden oat or giant feather
grass, *Stipa gigantea*. Originating
from the Iberian Peninsula, this
stately species forms durable, dark
green tussocks of narrow leaves
from which tall wands emerge
growing at least 2 metres high.
As the stems extend, papery,
hull-shaped flowers begin to
open in loose, shimmering
panicles. At first, the flower parts
are pale, silvery green but as they
mature, they take on a metallic
bronze hue before subsiding to
beige in late summer. When
planted so that the flower stems
can be seen with the light behind
them, the effect is dazzling and,
since such plants are open
in habit, one can easily look
through the narrow stems to
the garden beyond.

mixed borders

The double Mixed Borders are one of Wisley's main attractions. Their vast size – each one 128 metres long and 6 metres wide – and position, running down the gentle slope from Battleston Hill towards lower gardens, gives them pride of place. Planting such vast beds presents a considerable challenge, not only to look spectacular in high summer, but to sustain their beauty from mid-spring to late autumn. The gauntlet is readily taken up, however, by Super-intendent of Floral Ornamental, David Jewell. His task is to compose planting schemes where colours, textures and statures are composed to create a lasting and changing floral symphony.

Every square metre of the mixed borders exhibits what Gertrude Jekyll used to call a 'flowery moment'. Here, North American purple cone flower, *Echinacea purpurea*, contrasts with sprays of white mugwort, *Artemisia lactiflora* 'Ghuizu Group', and the filigree foliage of *Eupatorium capillifolium*.

(ABOVE) Hot and cool contrasts here with red *Crocosmia* 'Lucifer' glowing beneath a tall meadow rue, *Thalictrum* 'Elin'. The vivid blue *Delphinium* 'Michael Ayres' peers over at right.

(RIGHT) *Dahlia* 'Nargold', is a medium-sized cactus type whose tubular ray florets are semi-fimbriated, which means they are partially split.

(ABOVE) Warm summer hues from
the bold leaves of *Canna* 'Phasion'
with the mahogany flowers of *Helenium*
'Bruno' in the foreground and yellow
H. 'Sonnenwunder' behind. The tall grass
is *Miscanthus sinensis* 'Zebrinus'.

(LEFT) Runner beans grown on tall supports. The variety is 'Wisley Magic', part of the RHS Bicentenary Collection of plant varieties.

(RIGHT) Healthy crops growing in the Model Vegetable Garden. The soil is low in natural fertility and demands regular dressings of compost to sustain good structure.

the model vegetable garden

Increasing numbers of people want to grow their own food, either on allotments or in their back gardens, so it is hardly surprising that interest in the kitchen gardens and fruit orchards at Wisley has never been stronger. Seeing such superb crops grown so professionally might prove daunting to beginner gardeners, but that is not the intention here. Rather, it is to show what can be done, on a small or medium scale, in conditions that are less than ideal. The sandy soil, in this part of Surrey, tends to be thin, fast-draining and hungry – easy to work, but not good for producing heavy crops.

As a result of excellent husbandry, however, chard, lettuce, leeks, potatoes and sweet corn are thriving here. Netting and fine mesh is used for protecting susceptible crops from bird attack and from cabbage white butterflies. Using barrier methods like this eliminates the need to resort to chemical sprays.

Besides being productive, a well-tended kitchen garden can look as beautiful as a flower border, when the crops are carefully placed. Climbing vegetables can be trained up supports and placed in prominent positions, to bring height and extra flower colour.

a collection of heathers

Much of the land around Wisley is sandy with acidic soil creating natural heathland conditions. Gorse abounds, in open landscapes, often with wild heathers, so it is hardly surprising that the species *Erica*, *Calluna* and *Daboecia* all grow well in this garden.

Wisley holds one of the NCCPG National Collections of *Erica* with 552 different varieties, and when one sees them grown in close association, it is easy to recognise their outstanding value as garden plants. Their low-growing, weed-suppressing habit, durability, evergreen foliage and brilliantly colourful flowers make them a supreme choice for ground cover, particularly in a low-maintenance garden. Different species flower at different times and many have distinctive foliage, so the right mix of heathers gives perennial pleasure.

The main picture shows bright heather flowers sparkling in fresh morning sunlight, with white-flowered *Erica vagans* 'Lyonesse', one of the many varieties of Cornish heath, in the foreground, flanked on its right by *Erica tetralix* 'Pink Star', a garden selection of a common British native, cross-leaved heath – so-named because the tiny leaves are in a cross formation up the stem. To the right, the vivid purple blooms of *Daboecia cantabrica* 'Harlequin', Saint Dabeoc's heath, almost overshadow all the heathers around it.

Calluna vulgaris 'Silver Rose'

Calluna vulgaris 'Apollo'

Daboecia cantabrica 'Harlequin'

Erica vagans 'Lyonesse'

the mediterranean border

Dark-centred, purple-blue daisy flowers of the South African *Berkheya purpurea* associate sweetly with the pale grey, button-head blooms of the South American *Eryngium eburneum* in this arid-style planting. The spidery yellow flowers of *Asphodeline liburnica* last but a morning whereas in the background, creamy white flower spikes of *Yucca filamentosa* last for weeks among the spiky evergreen leaves. Maturing seed heads of the garlic relative, *Nectaroscordum siculum* are visible on the right.

(LEFT) Despite coming from disparate regions of the world, these plants associate well together to create a cosmopolitan mix, because they originate from similar hot, dry habitats.

(ABOVE) A dogwood, *Cornus kousa* var. *chinensis* 'Wisley Queen' in full glory. Handsome fruits will follow, and the autumn foliage display, in a favourable year, is magnificent.

weather hill

A collection of trees suitable for small and medium-sized gardens has been selected for year-round interest. Some have attractive blossom or fruit, others interesting bark or good leaf colour, but in certain outstanding examples, many of these qualities occur on the same plant. The ornamental dogwoods are a fine example, as are certain flowering cherries, crab apples, maples and hawthorns.

(ABOVE) Silvers, greys and duns create a soft, late-summer atmosphere in the Glasshouse Borders with Miss Willmott's Ghost, *Eryngium giganteum* 'Silver Ghost', in the foreground, backed by dying stems of the grass *Calamagrostis* x *acutiflora* 'Karl Foerster'. Other species of sea holly, *Eryngium*, appear among the grasses.

(RIGHT) A New World sea holly, *Eryngium yuccifolium* contrasts colour, texture and shape with the intense violet-blue of *Perovskia atriplicifolia* 'Little Spire'.

the glasshouse borders

In contrast to the traditional formality of the Mixed Borders, the acclaimed Dutch plantsman and designer Piet Oudolf was invited to create these modern naturalistic perennial plantings. Over 16,000 perennials and grasses are planted here in an arrangement of more than 30 diagonal 'rivers' of three or four cultivars. Taking his inspiration from prairie plantings, Piet chose species and cultivars with an open, airy feel to give the impression of walking in a meadow.

These borders have a long period of interest and are only cut down in late January. In winter, the stems of the perennials give structure and interest, and they also provide a haven for birds and other wildlife.

(OVERLEAF) An ocean of echinaceas paints a bold sweep of late summer purples, a theme that is picked up, further back, by another North American perennial, *Monarda*.

the torrid zone

In the Subtropical Border, adjacent to the Model Gardens, bold, fast-growing foliage is deployed to conjure up a sense of the exotic. You could expect to find an almost identical planting scheme in Barbados, Bali or Singapore! Cannas are the star performers, here, topping their broad, oval, glossy foliage with brilliant blooms that keep on opening until summer is over. Varieties like *Canna* 'Phasion', in the foreground, deliver a double bonus, with richly striped foliage as well as orange flowers, and C. 'Verdi' teams intense scarlet-orange flowers with bronze foliage.

The huge leaves of the Ethiopian native *Ensete ventricosum* – a close relative of the banana – make strong but temporary architecture in the background, contrasting their deep green colour with the grey-green, divided leaves of cardoons, *Cynara cardunculus*. Rooted suckers of the tree of heaven, *Ailanthus altissima*, and a *Paulownia tomentosa*, pollarded to stimulate growth of huge leaves, complete the verdure. Hot-hued flowers such as the Mexican torch, *Tithonia rotundifolia*, dot the scene with extra colour.

Although they look permanent and durable, these glories last but a summer. Most of the plants are tender and will not survive a British winter unless protected. Banana plants could be wrapped up or lagged *in situ*, but most plants will have to be lifted and held over in a greenhouse.

(ABOVE) The Walled Garden East in the
height of summer.

the walled gardens

In the Walled Garden East, the planting scheme shows how magnificent formal bedding can be when the annual *Rudbeckia hirta* is used in massed planting. High walls create a sun-trap, here, ensuring a long run of colour from the dark selection 'Golden Brown' and the warm yellow 'Indian Summer', as well as from the contrasting purple of the intensely fragrant *Heliotropium arborescens* 'Marine'. Silvery yellow-green bands of *Helichrysum petiolare* 'Limelight' provide a contrasting edge to the main beds, and tall specimens of castor oil plant *Ricinus communis* 'Carmencita' and *Canna* 'Roi Humbert' are placed as dot plants. Sweet potato, *Ipomoea batatas* 'Rudolf,' grows in the urn, along with cannas and yet more rudbeckias.

(RIGHT) *Rudbeckia hirta* 'Toto' is one of the best varieties for persistent flowering, compact habit and a strong contrast between the outer ray florets and dark central cone.

The Walled Garden West, in contrast, has an informal planting, where the near-hardy Japanese banana (*Musa basjoo*) arches over a sunlit path creating a hot, tropical feel. Such large, pendent leaves are doubly effective when light is seen shining through them, creating dark shadows that dance in the breeze. Strong winds, however, can split or even shred the fragile leaf tissue. Cordylines and New

(ABOVE) Neither a palace courtyard in Morocco nor a Moorish garden in Spain – simply part of the Walled Gardens at Wisley.

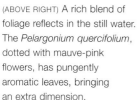

(ABOVE RIGHT) A rich blend of foliage reflects in the still water. The *Pelargonium quercifolium*, dotted with mauve-pink flowers, has pungently aromatic leaves, bringing an extra dimension.

Zealand flaxes (*Phormium*) further enhance the exotic ambience, and at this time of year they hold stiffly branched flower stems high above their foliage.

At the water's edge, green, cane-like stems of Dutch rush, *Equisetum hyemale*, make an upright contrast with the softer, broader foliage on either side.

autumn

autumn leaves

Slanting sunlight and gentle decay, in the autumn garden, creates a delicious melancholy – a mood to be enjoyed, rather than regretted – like a cello playing a seductive melody in a minor key. You know the colours cannot last and that the days are shortening, but you welcome the passing of the season.

In the Rock Garden, this specimen of *Acer palmatum* var. *heptalobum* has matured to a stately tree, presiding over its temporary carpet of fallen leaves. In late winter, long after those leaves have decayed, the ground beneath the spreading branches will be carpeted with drifts of *Cyclamen coum* whose dark, marbled leaves contrast with the vivid carmine flowers.

(ABOVE) The 80 year-old bonsai *Acer palmatum*, in the Garden of the Senses, demonstrates the natural form of a mature tree, scaled down.

(LEFT) Autumn leaves of *Cotinus obovatus*, the American smoke tree.

(ABOVE) Seven Acres, which until 1920 was rough pasture land, is planted with large specimen trees; one of the finest is *Nyssa sylvatica* 'Wisley Bonfire', seen here in the background.

Three elements that work together, in a well-tempered garden, are structure, colour and light. The most dominant structure in Seven Acres, the Chinese Pavilion, makes a startling focal point and looks almost incongruous, among the greenery of an essentially English setting. But the large trees temper its effect, especially when they are so warm in their autumn colours.

In the Garden of the Senses – a Model Garden donated to Wisley by Dawn and Peter Chan – the dominant structure is a small but ancient tree, looking its best when back-lit by a slanting autumn sun.

Persian ironwood, *Parrotia persica*, a large, spreading tree prized for its autumn colour.

forgotten flowers

Most of us associate flowers with spring or summer, but the autumn flora can be richer and more colourful. Many species carry internal clocks, which hold back blooming until days are growing noticeably shorter. Then, they burst forth with a flourish, flowering in profusion, hurrying to seed before winter.

Others have multiple seasons. *Clematis* 'Helios' flowers on old wood, in early summer, and again, on new growth until autumn. Earlier flowers develop silky seed heads whose texture contrasts with the 'lemon peel' blossoms as well as with the scarlet flowers of *Lobelia cardinalis* 'Queen Victoria'.

AUTUMN DAISES

Wild asters, garnered over the centuries from both the Old World and the Americas, have been hybridised to provide a huge and diverse range of late-blooming perennials. Swiss breeder Carl Ludwig Frikart, for example, crossed *Aster thomsonii* and *A. amellus*, in the 1920s, to produce several world-class varieties. The elegant, violet-blue *Aster* x *frikartii* 'Wunder von Stäfa', below, is named after his nursery at Stäfa. Frikart's asters are prized for their clean colours and long flowering period.

Chrysanthemums are ancient Chinese garden plants whose wild ancestry has become obscured by time. Many centuries of breeding has resulted in a remarkable diversity in hardiness, habit and colour from huge-bloomed varieties for the florists' trade, or for competitions, to the durable 'Korean' chrysanthemums, shown opposite, whose masses of little flowers have great decorative impact in an autumn border.

Autumn borders work themselves into a floral frenzy, given enough sunshine, moisture and fertile soil. Shrub foliage may be looking a little tired by now, before it fires up for its late finale, but flower colours are never fresher nor more vibrant than among Michaelmas daisies, border chrysanthemums, dahlias or the bright prairie plants of North America and the Caucasus. A plantsman, painting his borders with flower colour is spoilt for choice, especially in the purple range.

(RIGHT) Most of the mauve hues in the Late Summer Borders come from *Aster amellus* cultivars, contrasting sharply with fiery chrysanthemums and the fine, straight stems of *Verbena bonariensis*.

(BELOW) The open habit of *Verbena bonariensis* enables it to stand tall in front of a blend of asters without obscuring their view. Such a planting provides a feast for late butterflies, stoking up with high-energy nectar before hibernation.

When days shorten, certain bulb and corm-bearing species produce flowers, often without visible foliage. Crocus-like in appearance but with larger, more distinctive flowers, the colchicums make bold splashes of colour, usually in bright lilac-mauve or pink tones. The Victorians called them 'naked ladies' or 'naked boys', on account of the leafless blossoms and, possibly, fleshy colours.

(BELOW) Meadow Saffron, *Colchicum autumnale*, is not a source of saffron, despite its name, and is the only *Colchicum* species to occur wild in Britain. Broad, bold foliage follows in spring.

(ABOVE) On Weather Hill, bare ground beneath an American yellowwood tree, *Cladrastis kentuckea*, is planted with the hybrid *Colchicum* 'Dick Trotter'.

...of mists and mellow fruitfulness

Ripening fruits, whether edible or not, make a decorative contribution to the autumn garden. The giant Himalayan lily, *Cardiocrinum giganteum*, has plump seed pods, which divide into three as they split to shed their tightly packed seed.

Some members of the cucumber and marrow family produce huge, showy and highly durable fruits in mellow colours, often with attractive shapes and protuberances. Orange-skinned pumpkins 'Atlantic Giant' and smaller 'Connecticut King' contrast with ribbed, green acorn squash and the diminutive, pale squash 'Little Boo'.

Ripening autumn fruits join the first autumnal tints in the trees. As well as the unusual fruits of *Cornus kousa* on Weather Hill, *Sorbus* berries appear in pink, white, orange, yellow and red throughout the garden. Birds love them, so they sometimes disappear

(ABOVE LEFT) Black Bryony, *Tamus communis*, is the only member of the yam family to grow wild in Britain. To some, a troublesome weed but to others this is a handsome climber with glossy foliage and vivid red berries.

(ABOVE) With its early display of spectacular white blossom, strawberry-like fruits and superb autumn leaf tints, *Cornus kousa* is one of the best all-season plants in cultivation.

quite early in the season, but generally the pink and white ones last longer. In the nearby rose catenary, you can find climbing and rambling roses with abundant bright rose hips. RHS members can apply for seed that is collected from RHS gardens.

the scent
of ripe apples

'Ingrid Marie' – late dessert variety bred in Denmark in 1910.

'Kidd's Orange Red' – a New Zealand-raised late dessert apple.

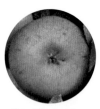

'Lord Derby'-type culinary variety.

The well-tended fruit orchards are a pleasure to visit at any time. Spring blossoms make an intense though brief flourish, but during autumn the apples swell, ripen and develop their characteristic colours, creating a mouth-watering array. Wisley has no fewer than 700 different varieties of apples, some of which – 'D'Arcy Spice', for example – date back many centuries. Visitors are welcome to wander among the trees, to compare the fruits and to see how different varieties perform.

The variety 'Gala' (main picture) is a dessert apple with luscious flavour and good colour, but to grow this well, the fruit trusses must be thinned and the tree skilfully pruned for maximum performance. At Wisley, the 'Gala' apples are ready for harvest in October.

(LEFT) Laid out in perfect symmetry, these rows of immaculately trained trees in Wisley's Fruit Field have often been described as a 'living library of apple cultivars'. As well as comparing the characteristics of individual varieties, one can also study the many different growing techniques used in the orchard.

(ABOVE) Apple 'Kidd's Orange Red'.

(BELOW) A ripening wild blackberry, *Rubus ulmifolius*.

The white bullace, whose flesh acquires a honey flavour when ripe. Traditionally, these were harvested in late autumn when the skin had begun to crack – hence the country name 'wintercracks'.

composing
with colour

When anyone refers to 'autumn tints' the colours that spring to mind are in the russet range. Falling leaves take on fiery tones and the green tends to drain out of many herbaceous plants whose foliage subsides to gold, beige or brown. But look more closely and you will find a wider range of subtle colour combinations, and many more seductive hues.

Ripening fruit, such as bullaces and damsons, undergo a series of colour changes from acid green, in July, through to their final hue when fully ripe. Damsons turn deep purple-black, but bullaces run through more gentle changes, often turning a pale, translucent amber.

Newly grown leaf rosettes of such biennials as foxgloves, mulleins or poppies develop fast in autumn, making a lively contrast with the dying foliage of dormant plants.

The sage green leaves of the Himalayan
poppy *Meconopsis napaulensis* are
covered with rusty gold hairs. Tall,
branched flower stems follow next year.

Decay can be beautiful. Changing colours and decomposing leaves are part of the natural process of decline, followed by winter rest and spring renewal. The reddening leaves of *Mahonia japonica* show a plant exhausted by a long, dry summer. Soon, fragrant blossoms will emerge from terminal buds, followed by fresh spring foliage. Even fallen leaves reward attention, running through colour changes as they rot, perhaps to leave a delicate network of bare veins.

(LEFT) Stress-induced colouring in *Mahonia japonica*, a winter-flowering shrub.

(BELOW) The decomposing leaf of *Liquidambar styraciflua*. As the green pigment chlorophyll breaks down, yellow and red pigments remain.

In the Monocot Borders at
Weather Hill, man-high stems
of *Yucca gloriosa* 'Variegata'
(above), smothered with big
creamy white bells, make a strong
contrast with the green and
cream stripes of the sharply
pointed leaves. The freshness
of that blossom stands out this
late in the season. In the grass
borders, however, colours of
the maturing flowers harmonise
more subtly in low-key tones
of soft, purplish browns, duns,
creams and silvery beige.

On the Grass Border in Seven Acres,
Miscanthus sinensis 'Rigoletto' (foreground,
left) is seen next to *Stipa calamagrostis*
with *Cortaderia selloana* towering above
it. In the centre background is purplish
Miscanthus sinensis 'Pünktchen'.

still waters

With a clear sky and calm weather, water reflects the bright hues of the surrounding trees. The deep, rusty red foliage of the dawn redwood, *Metasequoia glyptostroboides* (on the left of the picture, below) has a slightly more intense colour than the American swamp cypresses, *Taxodium distichum*. Both are deciduous conifers with soft, feathery needles. The central tree, forming a handsome, floating column, is the swamp cypress cultivar 'Nutans'.

On the more shaded side of the lake, a low sun lights up the trees from behind, enabling the mature specimen of *Nyssa sylvatica* (on the left of the picture, opposite) to live up to its cultivar name 'Wisley Bonfire'.

(RIGHT) The trees *Nyssa sylvatica* 'Wisley Bonfire', *Betula pendula* 'Dalecarlica', Scots pine and the willow *Salix magnifica* furnish the lake margin.

(BELOW) The lake at Seven Acres reflecting a tree-clad skyline.

On Seven Acres, the
thick tapering bole
of the dawn redwood,
*Metasequoia
glyptostroboides*,
a Chinese species
discovered in 1941,
balances by the tall
column of an upright
oak, *Quercus robur* f.
fastigiata.

The royal fern, *Osmunda regalis*, is a deciduous species whose pale green, sterile fronds take on the hue of old gold as they die. Spores are produced on adapted, fertile stems. At Wisley, it grows along water courses in the Wild Garden. Though fully hardy, this is a plant of acid wetlands and will not tolerate lime.

winter

the awakening year

Even in the depths of winter, the cycle of plant life is ready to begin again. Fractional increases in day length, after the solstice, can initiate growth and even flowering, particularly among dwarf winter bulbs. One cannot help but admire their pluck, especially when repeated frosts and chilling winds fail to damage those delicate-looking blooms. Snowdrops like these early-blooming *Galanthus elwesii*, their heads temporarily bowed by frost, can bloom from Christmas until winter's end. They make charming companions to the equally hardy *Cyclamen coum*.

One of the earliest species to flower, *Crocus tommasinianus* naturalises readily in grass. The outer tepals are pale grey, making the flowers almost invisible in the turf until sunshine opens them to reveal lilac-mauve interiors.

A rugged Caucasian species, *Cyclamen coum* is impervious
to hard frost, producing carmine, pink or white blossoms
from late December until March, accompanied by rounded,
marbled leaves.

sculpted by man, made by nature

A garden is reduced to its bare bones in winter, when structure and strong outlines become all important. Fine sculptures furnish various parts of the garden, but pride of place, at the top of Battleston Hill, is taken by an imposing Henry Moore. Mature trees also create their own natural sculptures, and when bare, they trace elegant outlines against the winter sky.

(ABOVE) Henry Moore's disturbingly life-like *The Arch*, 6 metres high and inspired by a fragment of bone.

(RIGHT) Nature's craft: Scots pines and an oak on Battleston Hill.

Salix alba
'Yelverton', a
willow prized for
its bright winter
twigs.

The colourful seeds of gladwyn, or roast beef plant, *Iris foetidissima*, persist for much of winter.

PLANT
PORTRAIT

WITCH HAZELS

Winter flowers are scarce and to be treasured when much of the colour, at this time of year, derives from such other sources as fruits, seeds, stems, bark and even dead foliage. Witch hazels are among the earliest shrubs to bloom, extending their spidery petals on mild days, but clenching them when cold. The best garden varieties arose from crossing the Japanese *Hamamelis japonica* with Chinese *H. mollis* to produce the hybrid *H.* x *intermedia*.

Hamamelis x *intermedia* 'Pallida' (left) is probably the best sulphur yellow cultivar available for garden use. It stands out well from a distance, and up close you can see the red-purple centres. The original specimen was planted on Battleston Hill sometime between 1941 and 1946, and you can find many other *H.* x *intermedia* cultivars around the Wild Garden, Pinetum and Seven Acres, such as 'Harry' (below) and 'Glowing Embers' (right).

tropic world in a surrey garden

How pleasant, on a freezing winter day, to take a few short paces
into the Wisley Glasshouse and enter one of the world's torrid
zones! The low humidity and high temperatures that suit such
desert plants as these are perfect for garden visitors in search of
a little warmth.

COMMON SOLUTION

Though totally unrelated, desert plants from diverse parts of the world have adapted to hot, arid conditions by developing strikingly similar characteristics.

Mexican native *Agave attenuata* produces, after several vegetative years, a large, long flower spike with an almost comical droop.

Though it originates from Africa, half a world away, the similarity of this species of *Aloe* to American agaves, is remarkable.

The century plant, *Agave americana* whose huge, branched flower spikes may be more than 8 metres tall, but which may take more than 30 years to appear.

(LEFt) A collection of bromeliads with the central fibre column planted with *Guzmania*. Old tree fern stems make excellent planting towers for bromeliads.

(right) *Hippeastrum* 'Amigo'.

Vibrant indoor displays are doubly attractive in winter, when outdoor colours tend to be muted. Luckily, there is a wide choice of tropical and subtropical plants that perform well in winter and among these, the bromeliads – members of the pineapple family – are particularly fine, having colourful leaves as well as flowers. Such winter-flowering bulbs as *Hippeastrum*, often incorrectly called 'amaryllis', are also effective, whether grown in large groups, or individually as windowsill plants.

(ABOVE) A view across the
Singapore Orchid House from
the main entrance.

(RIGHT) This *Calanthe* hybrid
belongs to a genus of variable
terrestrial orchids from Asia,

Polynesia and Madagascar. It
will be moved to a shadier
position in the summer.

life in transition

The plants illustrated on these pages were photographed in the original glasshouses, which, sadly, have reached the end of their useful lives. After a period of transition, the collection will be transferred, along with many new introductions, to the magnificent Bicentenary Glasshouse, opening in 2007. Their new home will be furnished with a much larger and more naturalistic landscape than in their old, rather cramped quarters, giving them the freedom to grow to the same dimensions as they might in their native habitats, be they from rainforest, deserts or temperate savannah.

(LEFT) Another genus of cool-growing orchids, *Cymbidium* is one of the easiest orchid types for amateur growers, and such varieties as 'Cooksbridge Satin', shown here, are superb as cut flowers.

(BELOW) A moth orchid *Phalaenopsis* grex 'Brother Lancer'. A 'grex', from the Latin meaning 'flock', refers to progeny from an artificial cross between known parents of different species.

(OPPOSITE) A hybrid *Odontoglossum*, one of the many hundreds in cultivation. Colours, besides pink tones, can include yellow and red. They prefer relatively cool conditions, since they are mountain plants from tropical South and Central America.

(ABOVE LEFT) *Cymbidium* King's Loch grex 'Cooksbridge'.
(ABOVE RIGHT) *Cymbidium* 'Highland Advent'.

Lime greens and pale yellows are widespread hues in this much-hybridised genus, often with dark red markings. Cymbidiums are large plants, with shocks of coarse, grassy foliage and can be rather ungainly in habit. Their flowers, produced in late winter or early spring, are remarkably long lasting, whether cut for arranging or left on the plants. After flowering, the plants can be placed outdoors, provided they are frost free.

(ABOVE LEFT) In the wild, more orchid species occur worldwide than any other plant family. Many are as beautiful, in their pure form, as when hybridised. From Central America, *Laelia anceps* is but one example, whose showy flowers vary in hue from rich rose purple, through shades of mauve-pink to white. Laelias have been used as breeding stock to develop a number of outstanding cultivated orchid varieties.

(ABOVE RIGHT) Another hybrid cymbidium, *C. Sandridge Torch 'Cindy'*, showing the pink to red colour range. Orchid hybrids are raised and registered in vast numbers, by both professional and amateur breeders. Only a select few stand the test of time.

Back-lit winter oaks, in the nacreous tones of a tea-time winter sunset. Such quiet beauty is as precious to recall as the brightest of midsummer scenes and shows that this, truly, is a garden for all seasons.

Back-lit winter oaks, in the nacreous tones of a tea-time winter sunset. Such quiet beauty is as precious to recall as the brightest of midsummer scenes and shows that this, truly, is a garden for all seasons.

index